WORLD WAR II

Why They Fought

BY KATIE MARSICO

CONTENT CONSULTANT
Cornelius L. Bynum, PhD
Associate Professor, Department of History
Purdue University

COMPASS POINT BOOKS
a capstone imprint

Compass Point Books are published by Capstone,
1710 Roe Crest Drive, North Mankato, Minnesota 56003
www.capstonepub.com

Editorial Credits
Melissa York, editor; Maggie Villaume, designer; Nikki Farinella, production specialist;
Catherine Neitge and Ashlee Suker, consulting editor and designer

Photo Credits
Corbis: 13, Bettmann/Corbis, 54; Keystone Pictures USA/Alamy, 46; Library of Congress: Ansel Adams, 30, Farm Security Administration/Office of War Information, 16, 39, Harris & Ewing, 19, U.S. Signal Corps, 50; U.S. National Archives and Records Administration: 58, 59, Franklin D. Roosevelt Library Public Domain Photographs, 17, 21, Office for Emergency Management/War Production Board, 31, U.S. Air Force, 53, U.S. Navy, 56, U.S. Office of War Information, 51; Naval History and Heritage Command, 37; Shutterstock Images: 5, Elzbieta Sekowska, 27, Everett Historical, 6, 23, 35; SuperStock: 11, Album, 9, Past Pix/SSPL/Science and Society, 8, 36, Schultz Reinhard/Prisma, 15, Science and Society, 43; U.S. Air Force, 42; U.S. Army Center of Military History, 44, 49; U.S. Marine Corps History Division: 25, 33, 41, Chamberlain, 29, Christian, cover

Library of Congress Cataloging-in-Publication Data
Marsico, Katie, 1980–
  World War II : why they fought / Katie Marsico.
     pages cm. — (What were they fighting for?)
  Includes bibliographical references and index.
  ISBN 978-0-7565-5171-1 (hardcover)
  ISBN 978-0-7565-5175-9 (paperback)
  ISBN 978-0-7565-5183-4 (ebook pdf)
  1. World War, 1939–1945—Juvenile literature. 2. World War, 1939–1945—Causes—Juvenile literature. I. Title.
  D743.7.M3615 2015
  940.53—dc23   2014045988

Printed in Canada.
032015   008825FRF15

TABLE OF CONTENTS

CHAPTER ONE
SEEDS
of War

The wounds from World War II still run deep. During the global conflict that raged from 1939 to 1945, society faced the terrifying effects of nuclear warfare and genocide. The war involved more than 60 countries and killed an estimated 60 million people. It pitted two groups of nations against one another. The Axis powers were led by Germany, Italy, and Japan. The United Kingdom, France, the United States, and the Soviet Union led the Allied powers.

Against the war's bloody backdrop, the daring and deadly decisions of the world's notable leaders had a huge impact. Seven decades later the world continues to ponder why the war began and what the combatants—both nations and individuals—were fighting for. The answer involves everything from economics and politics to a previous global crisis, World War I (1914–1918).

Political instability was at the root of several of the conflicts that shaped World War I. The war began with the assassination of the heir to the throne of Austria-Hungary. Multiple countries quickly divided into opposite camps. The Allied powers featured the United Kingdom, France, Russia, Belgium,

Memorials around the world help visitors remember the horrors of genocide from World War II's holocaust.

Many horrors of modern warfare, including poison gas, aerial bombing, and tanks, first appeared in World War I.

Italy, and the United States. Germany, Austria-Hungary, the Ottoman Empire (Turkey), and Bulgaria formed the backbone of the Central powers.

When World War I concluded, the Allies emerged victorious, though casualties from both sides totaled about 37 million. Until the next war engulfed the world, World War I was regarded as the deadliest conflict in history. The war saw the immense destruction that tanks, fighter planes, submarines, poison gas, and trench warfare could exact.

In Russia, a bloody revolution led to the execution of the Russian royal family in 1918. Later, Communist leaders took control of the government. Soon after, the Russian empire was carved into a group of republics that together formed the Soviet Union.

The Treaty of Versailles, which officially concluded World War I in 1919, stripped Germany of territory. It also forced the nation to reduce its military. In addition, Germans had to pay roughly $33 billion in reparations. Weighed down by this staggering debt, Germany struggled with inflation and unemployment.

A group of former Allied powers created the League of Nations in 1920. It was established to promote international peace and security. The era ahead would perhaps be peaceful. Yet it would be far from prosperous. Countries were in ruins and a generation was decimated. The hardships of the postwar era set the stage for political extremism. Leaders such as fascist Italian dictator Benito Mussolini rose to power in the early 1920s. Mussolini was determined to restore Italy to the greatness it had experienced in the days of the Roman Empire more than 1,500 years earlier.

In Germany fascist leader Adolf Hitler was similarly aggressive in his nationalism. Hitler developed the National Socialist German Workers' Party—known as the Nazi Party—in the 1920s. The Nazis believed they had an unquestionable right to expand their country's borders. Their ultimate goal was to restore Germany's status as a major world power. The Nazis thought the strength of their nation lay in the racial purity of the German people. To the Germans, racial purity meant ensuring white, Christian,

"For today Germany belongs to us, and tomorrow, the whole world."

—Nazi Party Song

heterosexual people of German ancestry, the so-called Aryan people, did not mix with people of different backgrounds or races. They believed Aryan people were superior to all others. Ultimately, Nazi ambitions drew much of Europe into World War II in an effort to stop them.

In the meantime Germany's financial troubles and political turmoil grew worse. The Great Depression, a worldwide economic crisis, had erupted in 1929. That year the U.S. stock market crashed. A dramatic slump in industry and employment followed. The crippling effects of the Great Depression spread poverty and hopelessness on a global scale. Germany was hit hard. Even the winners of World War I were not immune, and tensions rose especially high in areas affected by political instability.

Hitler was named chancellor of Germany in 1933. For many Germans, Hitler's rise to power made it possible to envision a brighter future. His passionate speeches allowed Germans

Adolf Hitler led with a mix of charisma and fear.

Japan increased its military during the 1930s.

to see beyond the bitter memory of losing World War I.

Meanwhile, Japan was also undergoing changes in leadership. A growing number of government officials were also high-ranking military officers. Like Hitler and Mussolini, these men wanted to create a vast empire.

Nationalist pride drove their quest for expansion, as well as a desire for more land and resources. After World War I, Japan watched as nations including the United States and the United Kingdom forged trade agreements in China and other parts of Asia. The Japanese depended on exports from these areas.

Japanese leaders believed they had more right to a Pacific empire than the United States and Europe did.

Japan took the first steps toward expansion in 1931. That year it invaded Manchuria in northeastern China—a region with key resources such as iron and coal. Several members of the League of Nations disapproved, and in 1933 Japan withdrew from the league. It was clear the Japanese were willing to fight for their vision of a new empire. Within a few years, Japan and China were in the midst of a full-scale war. China would suffer terrible casualties before the war's end, with at least 20 million mostly civilian deaths.

The United States, the United Kingdom, France, and the Netherlands were uneasy about Japanese aggression. The four nations controlled territory in the Pacific Ocean and throughout Southeast Asia. At the same time, however, no one was eager to become involved in another global conflict. Many people were also more focused on economic recovery in the midst of the Great Depression.

But it was difficult to ignore the heightened tensions taking shape in other areas. Mussolini invaded Ethiopia in northern Africa in 1935. Three years later Hitler's troops annexed Austria. Not long afterward Hitler insisted that Germany had a rightful claim to a part of Czechoslovakia known as the Sudetenland. The region was home to roughly 3 million ethnic Germans.

The British and French knew Hitler had been rebuilding the German army, which violated the Treaty of Versailles. Hitler had organized 500,000 troops by 1935. Anxious to protect the European peace, British Prime Minister Neville Chamberlain and French officials signed the Munich Pact in September

Neville Chamberlain hoped his agreement with Hitler would prevent war. ▶

1938. According to the agreement, the United Kingdom and France would not oppose Hitler's occupation of the Sudetenland. In turn, Hitler would not demand more territory. After signing the Munich Pact, Chamberlain gave a hopeful speech in London, England.

"My good friends," said Chamberlain, "this is the second time in our history that there has come back from Germany ... peace with honour. I believe it is peace for our time. We thank you from the bottom of our hearts ... And now I recommend you go home and sleep quietly in your beds."

By early 1939, however, it became obvious that the Munich Pact had failed. The Sudetenland was not enough to satisfy Germany. In March Hitler invaded the rest of Czechoslovakia. Next he insisted on the right to annex portions of Poland. As Hitler reached for more of Europe, world leaders were forced to react to his aggression. Italy formed an alliance with Germany, while the United Kingdom and France vowed to support Poland's independence.

If the Germans annexed Poland, their empire would reach the Soviet Union's western border. Soviet leader Joseph Stalin was unlikely to stand by and do nothing while the Germans swarmed into eastern Europe. Hitler knew it would be difficult to win a war on two fronts. Thus the Nazis held secret talks with the Soviets in August 1939 that resulted in the Nonaggression Pact. The Soviet Union and Germany agreed not to fight each other or support each other's enemies. They also discussed how they would divide eastern Europe after Hitler's invasion of Poland.

More than 1.5 million German troops rushed over the Polish border in a blitzkrieg attack on September 1. *Blitzkrieg* is German for "lightning," and, like lightning, Hitler's offensive was swift and powerful. He relied

Hitler's invasion of Poland was a threat to the rest of Europe.

on tanks, planes, and submarines to strike Poland on land, in the air, and at sea. When Hitler refused to leave Poland, the United Kingdom and France declared war on Germany on September 3. The conflict that would forever change the continent of Europe was officially under way.

CHAPTER TWO
EUROPE
Under Attack

" I have said this before, but I shall say it again and again and again; your boys are not going to be sent into any foreign wars." So spoke U.S. President Franklin D. Roosevelt as he addressed the nation in fall 1940. Americans were still reeling from both World War I and the Great Depression. They hoped to limit their involvement in World War II.

Neutrality became unrealistic for the United Kingdom and France. British and French leaders had signed the Munich Pact to preserve peace. Yet, since 1939, Hitler had defied the terms of the agreement. He and Stalin had overrun Poland by late September 1939 and were splitting it up. The war had begun.

The Soviet Union invaded Finland in late November. Then, in the spring, Germany stormed into Denmark and Norway. In May Hitler also ordered his troops to attack France, Luxembourg, the Netherlands, and Belgium. The Germans clearly intended to occupy western Europe.

Winston Churchill replaced Neville Chamberlain as the British prime minister in early May. Churchill explained the new British policy to the House of Commons. "It is to wage war,

Und Ihr habt doch gesiegt!

Propaganda urged on the German people as Hitler moved to occupy Europe. The postcard's text translates as "And you were victorious after all."

by sea, land and air, with all our might ... to wage war against a monstrous tyranny ... You ask, what is our aim? I can answer with one word: It is victory, victory at all costs, victory in spite of all terror, victory however long and hard the road may be; for without victory, there is no survival."

Churchill wasn't exaggerating the crisis his nation faced in 1940. The Nazis were intent on conquering the European continent, and their ambitions were a serious threat to the United Kingdom. It was crucial that the British halt German aggression in western Europe. Otherwise, they would be overrun too. British soldiers and people at home all knew what they were fighting for: the survival of their nation.

The United Kingdom led a massive evacuation of British, French, and Belgian forces from Dunkirk, France, later in May. The Allies fended off assaults from the German air force, the Luftwaffe, as they rescued 340,000 soldiers. A few weeks afterward, the French and Germans reached a temporary agreement. In exchange for an end to hostilities, Hitler occupied northern France and some Atlantic coastline.

Though the French were no longer officially at war with the Axis powers, many still found ways to oppose the Nazis. They formed small groups that

Prime Minister Winston Churchill asked the British people to be strong and brave through German attacks.

The Blitz brought terrible destruction to London.

were together known as the French Resistance. Some French Resistance groups attacked German troops. Others circulated secret newspapers and radio broadcasts to urge the French to keep fighting.

Meanwhile, the British knew Hitler had no intention of halting at their borders. The Germans launched a 57-day assault on London on September 7 that became known as the Blitz. The Nazis planned to bring British civilians to their knees with intense Luftwaffe air raids.

While working in London in 1940, U.S. journalist Ernie Pyle recorded vivid accounts of what he witnessed during the Blitz: "the monstrous loveliness of ... London stabbed with great fires, shaken by explosions ... all of it roofed over with a ceiling of pink that held bursting shells, balloons, flares, and the grind of vicious engines ... These things all went together to make the most hateful, most beautiful single scene I have ever known."

Hitler's actions won him new allies. Italy and Japan signed the Tripartite Pact with Germany on September 27. It outlined formal alliances between the countries that made up the Axis powers. The pact demonstrated Axis support for Germany's attack on the United Kingdom. It was also a warning to the United States. At that point many Americans still regarded World War II as a largely European war. The United States had adopted an official policy during the 1930s of remaining isolated from foreign conflicts. Many believed the vast oceans would protect them. In addition, some military leaders thought it was important to conserve U.S. resources. They pointed out that the United States might not remain neutral forever. However, Americans were partners in a long-standing alliance with the British. The diplomatic friendship made it difficult to refuse when Churchill requested help. Nor did the spread of fascism sit well with U.S. citizens, who enjoyed the freedoms of a democratic government.

The United States also remained wary of Japan's desire to colonize the Pacific. U.S. troops had already evacuated Americans from war-torn areas in China. The United States and other Allied nations answered Japanese aggression with trade restrictions starting in the late 1930s. They believed reducing oil, steel, and iron exports might help stop Japan's expansion.

Roosevelt considered the issues while addressing the nation on December 29, 1940. "If Great Britain goes down, the Axis powers will control the continents of Europe, Asia, Africa, Australasia, and the high seas ... All of us, in all the Americas, would be living at the point of a gun—a gun loaded with explosive bullets, economic as well as military ... For us this is an emergency as serious as war itself."

A growing number of U.S. citizens were beginning to see the wisdom of Roosevelt's words. Not all of them were prepared to declare war or send troops overseas. Yet the threat of Axis influence loomed large. It was unclear how much longer the United States would be able to avoid fighting.

WARTIME LEADER

Franklin Delano Roosevelt was born January 30, 1882, in Hyde Park, New York. The son of wealthy parents, Roosevelt was privately tutored as a child. He married distant cousin Eleanor Roosevelt, niece of President Theodore Roosevelt, in 1905. He won a seat in the state senate in 1910 and was re-elected in 1912. Then, from 1913 to 1920, he served as assistant secretary of the navy.

In 1921 he caught polio—a paralyzing illness that confined him to a wheelchair. Yet Roosevelt didn't let this challenge stand in the way of his political career. After serving as governor of New York from 1928 to 1932, he ran for U.S. president and won. He was re-elected in 1936, 1940, and 1944, the only U.S. president to serve more than two four-year terms. He frequently addressed the nation by radio as he led the nation through the dark days of World War II. He is also remembered for his New Deal legislation, which created jobs and provided other economic relief during the Great Depression. Roosevelt suffered a fatal stroke at the age of 63 on April 12, 1945. His death occurred shortly before World War II drew to a close.

CHAPTER THREE

INVASIONS of 1941

Franklin Roosevelt pushed forward with his goal of making the United States a "great arsenal of democracy." He introduced a bill to Congress in January 1941 that became the basis of the Lend-Lease Act. It allowed the U.S. government to provide arms and supplies to countries it thought were vital to U.S. defense. In turn, nations including the United Kingdom promised to repay whatever they borrowed at a later date.

Congress passed the Lend-Lease Act in March. Some Americans were still hesitant about the United States' growing involvement in World War II.

Yet others perceived the Lend-Lease Act as a necessary measure. They argued that while the British held the Germans back, the United States could better prepare for the possibility of war. The United States also increased military production at its factories and plants. Men between the ages of 21 and 45 registered for the United States' first peacetime draft. U.S. ships started transporting military supplies.

Meanwhile, Hitler violated the terms of the Nonaggression Pact in June and invaded the Soviet Union. Why did Hitler break the agreement? For the first few years of the war, the

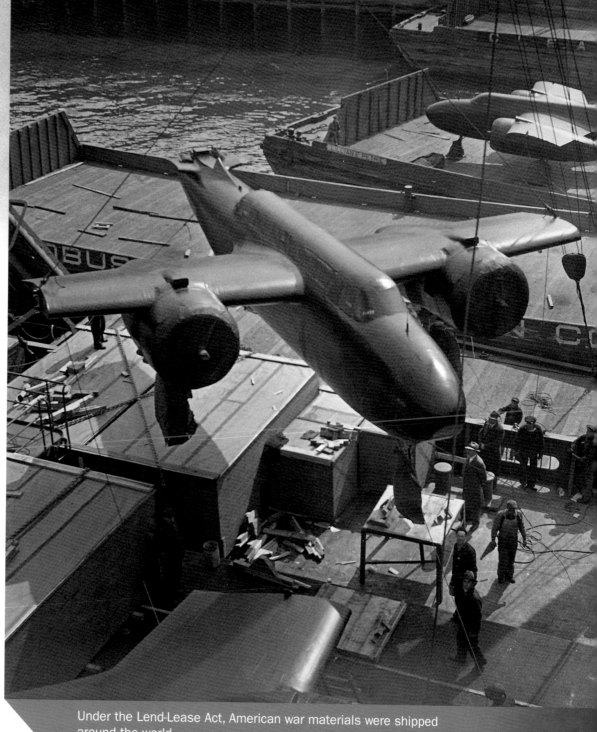

Under the Lend-Lease Act, American war materials were shipped around the world.

Nazis had been mostly successful in their occupation of Europe. The Soviets hadn't interfered during Germany's campaign in Poland, so Hitler's pact with Stalin had already served its primary purpose. Since 1939 Stalin's Red Army had busily occupied eastern Europe. Apart from the Nonaggression Pact, there was little to guarantee the Soviets wouldn't turn on Germany next. Besides, Hitler's vision of a powerful German empire depended on acquiring more and more territory. Occupying the United Kingdom wasn't going to be enough. Hitler and his officials therefore believed that the Soviets represented a more pressing problem than the British.

One of Hitler's generals later explained the strategy. "We knew that in two years' time, that is by the end of 1942 [or the] beginning of 1943, the English would be ready, the Americans would be ready, the Russians would be ready, too, and then we would have to deal with all three of them at the same time ... We had to try to remove the greatest threat from the East ... At the time, it seemed possible."

Initially, it looked as though the Germans' blitzkrieg assaults would pave the way to victory in the Soviet Union. After years of enduring Stalin's iron-fisted rule, some Soviet citizens even welcomed Hitler's troops. But the German occupation failed to improve their situation. As the Germans inched closer to Moscow, the Soviets' capital city, Stalin pushed back with steely determination. He refused to flee Moscow, and he ordered that anyone who tried to leave be shot.

The Russian people were essentially trapped in what quickly became a deadly situation. Residents of the Soviet Union fought as much out of fear and desperation as patriotic pride. By the time World War II concluded, roughly 24 million Soviets were dead. Those who were not slaughtered

The Nazis first used concentration camps to detain their enemies for forced labor beginning in 1933. As the terrible system evolved, camps also became the site of the mass killing of millions of people.

outright often died of starvation or disease. In other cases Soviet prisoners of war (POWs) were relocated to Nazi concentration camps. Life in concentration camps was harsh. Illness and hunger were widespread, as were forced labor and beatings. It was not unusual for prisoners to be executed for no reason.

Concentration camps imprisoned Jews, Roman Catholics, people with disabilities, and anyone who didn't fit into or share Nazi ideologies. What began as labor camps transformed into a terrible system of extermination camps focused on eliminating Jews from Europe. The countless crimes against humanity that occurred in the camps would gain international attention in years to come.

In 1941, however, much of the world was more attuned to Germany's

Soviet invasion. The Soviet Union joined the Allies after Hitler's attack. Roosevelt dispatched Lend-Lease aid to the Soviets in October. Soon the United States would be compelled to take a more direct stand against the Axis powers.

The previous summer Japan had invaded French Indochina (Vietnam, Laos, and Cambodia). Within days the United States, the United Kingdom, and the Netherlands responded by refusing to conduct business with Japan. The result was that the Japanese couldn't easily buy oil.

U.S. leaders weren't inclined to go to war to halt Japanese expansion. But they also weren't willing to lift trade restrictions. Faced with this stalemate, the Japanese planned to invade parts of Southeast Asia to secure a new oil supply. But first they had to deal with a major roadblock, the U.S. naval fleet in the Pacific.

Japanese Prime Minister Tojo Hideki's solution was a devastating surprise attack on Pearl Harbor, the U.S. naval base on the island of Oahu in Hawaii. Japanese pilots bombed Pearl Harbor on December 7, 1941. The assault cost 2,403 Americans their lives and caused considerable damage to the U.S. fleet. A day later Roosevelt addressed Congress to request a declaration of war. Congress declared war on Japan on December 8.

Following the bombing of Pearl Harbor, thousands of Americans signed up to serve their country. The United States would

> **"I enlisted after Pearl Harbor ... I quit college ... There was a great uproar in the country then, and everybody was full of patriotic fervor."**
>
> —U.S. Coast Guard member

The USS *Helena* was damaged but stayed afloat during the attack on Pearl Harbor. ▶

Principal Allied, Axis, and Neutral Nations, 1942

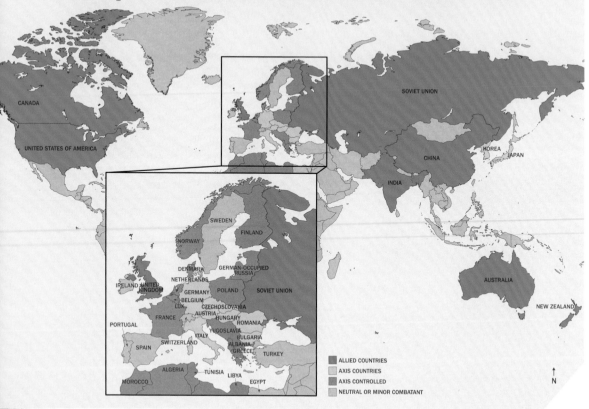

CANADA

UNITED STATES OF AMERICA

SOVIET UNION

KOREA

JAPAN

CHINA

INDIA

SWEDEN

NORWAY

FINLAND

DENMARK

GERMAN-OCCUPIED RUSSIA

NETHERLANDS

IRELAND

UNITED KINGDOM

GERMANY

POLAND

SOVIET UNION

BELGIUM

LUX.

CZECHOSLOVAKIA

FRANCE

AUSTRIA

HUNGARY

ROMANIA

PORTUGAL

ITALY

YUGOSLAVIA

BULGARIA

SWITZERLAND

ALBANIA

GREECE

TURKEY

SPAIN

ALGERIA

TUNISIA

LIBYA

EGYPT

MOROCCO

AUSTRALIA

NEW ZEALAND

ALLIED COUNTRIES

AXIS COUNTRIES

AXIS CONTROLLED

NEUTRAL OR MINOR COMBATANT

N

depend on such dedication in the days to come. At about the same time, Japanese troops stormed into other locations throughout the Pacific. The United States needed its full military might to meet the threat.

Germany and Italy declared war on the United States on December 11 in support of their ally. Beyond honoring the alliance, overcoming U.S. forces appealed to Hitler for other reasons. The United States was interfering with his plans for western Europe by supplying the United Kingdom. Hitler likely suspected that the United States would soon declare war on Germany. The war was growing, and the reasons for fighting were shifting.

THE RUTHLESS RULER OF NAZI GERMANY

Adolf Hitler was born April 20, 1889, in Braunau am Inn, Austria. He dropped out of school in 1905 and began working as a painter and laborer. During the years ahead, Hitler struggled financially and even lived in a homeless shelter. He signed up to serve in the German army in 1914. Later he was honored for his bravery in World War I.

That conflict had a deep impact on Hitler, who was bitterly disappointed by Germany's surrender. In the postwar years he became increasingly involved in politics. He ran for president in 1932 and lost but was ultimately appointed chancellor. Before long, Hitler's political influence and passionate nationalism effectively allowed him to rule Germany. His Nazi Party controlled the country by 1933.

Following Hitler's rise to power, Germany entered World War II, an era of fear and persecution in the country. Hitler executed countless individuals whom he considered a threat to the racial purity of the German people. As the war drew to a close, however, Allied forces overcame the Nazis. Hitler went into hiding in an underground bunker in Berlin, Germany, in the spring of 1945. He and his wife, Eva Braun, committed suicide in their secret shelter on April 30.

CHAPTER FOUR
WARTIME
Experiences

American troops were traveling to places across the globe by early 1942. Some headed to the United Kingdom, while others traveled to locations in the Pacific. German forces kept much of Europe in their grip. Hitler's U-boat submarines began attacking U.S. ships in the Atlantic. The United States also faced problems in the Pacific. During the first few months of 1942, Allied nations suffered staggering losses in the Java Sea and the Philippines. The mountains, jungles, and swamps of many Pacific islands made it difficult to transport food and supplies.

After the bombing of Pearl Harbor, Americans' sense of security was deeply shaken. Fear of another attack led to widespread paranoia. U.S. citizens of Japanese, German, and Italian ancestry were frequently suspected of being spies or traitors. It was especially true for anyone with ties to Japan. The U.S. government started ordering Japanese-Americans into internment camps in February 1942. Similar to prison camps, the heavily guarded areas eventually held more than 117,000 people until they closed at the end of the war. U.S. officials described the internment camps as

Many U.S. Marines fought in the Pacific.

Japanese families had no choice but to relocate to remote camps.

safeguards against possible disloyalty in the event that Japan invaded. For the most part, however, few residents had ever given any indication of treachery. Japanese-Americans had to fight to demonstrate their allegiance to the United States and regain their freedoms as citizens.

As World War II progressed, rationing became commonplace in Allied and Axis nations alike. Factories changed production to provide overseas troops with weapons and supplies. People on the home front received stamps that they used to buy goods. They also planted victory gardens to put less strain on public food production.

The organizational and economic skills of women on the home front helped rationing succeed. With their

> **"Shivering in the cold, we pressed close together ... I felt degraded, humiliated, and overwhelmed with a longing for home. And I saw the unutterable sadness on my mother's face."**
>
> —Yoshiko Uchida's recollections of Tanforan, an assembly center in California where internees gathered to go to camps

fathers, husbands, and brothers serving in the military, many women faced new roles and responsibilities. They had to create effective household budgets based on limited resources. Women also took over factory positions and other jobs that had once been held mostly by men.

During the early 1940s, the image of Rosie the Riveter became a cultural icon in the United States. Rosie was often depicted in art with her sleeves rolled back and a determined expression on her face. She represented the fierce battle women were waging to support overseas troops and U.S. industry. The female citizens of nations such as the United Kingdom and the Soviet Union demonstrated similar dedication during World War II.

Lydia Vladimirovna Litvyak gained fame in the Soviet Union as a female fighter pilot. Nicknamed the White Rose of Stalingrad, Litvyak shot down 14 enemy planes. U.S. military

forces reflected impressive female involvement as well. Almost 350,000 women served in the U.S. military in World War II. Many were nurses. Other military women held office jobs, drove

Rosie the Riveter inspired U.S. women to get to work.

trucks, worked in laboratories, and flew or repaired planes. They offered up their time and talent—and occasionally their lives—to support their country. Many also hoped that enlisting would provide new training and career opportunities. After the war, however, most lost their military jobs to men returning from combat.

Racial discrimination had stood in the way of African-Americans piloting military planes during World War I. In World War II the pilots at last had an opportunity to disprove popular prejudices. The United States activated the 99th Pursuit Squadron—better known as the Tuskegee Airmen. The Tuskegee Airmen made up the first all-African-American unit of the U.S. Army Air Corps. Though African-American pilots still faced unequal treatment, they demonstrated their skill, talent, and patriotism. As the war progressed, the Tuskegee Airmen damaged or destroyed hundreds of enemy aircraft, railcars, ships, boats, and barges.

African-American military members served bravely throughout the war. Doris Miller, a navy cook, operated a machine gun during the attack on Pearl Harbor. He received high honors. The Double V Campaign on the home front encouraged African-Americans to do all they could for the war effort while at the same time urging the government to increase racial equality.

Many African-Americans who participated in World War II did not receive the same national support as whites. Nor did they consistently enjoy equal recognition and opportunities following the war. But their battle to chip away at prejudice and discrimination was not in vain. They fought to protect their country and demonstrate that skin color did not determine intelligence, strength, or loyalty.

REMARKABLE WARTIME MESSENGERS

During World War II, military officials relied heavily on phone and radio communication. But spies were always listening, so it was dangerous to discuss details such as the location of troops or combat strategies. As a result, military communication frequently involved complex codes. Both Allied and Axis nations employed highly trained code breakers to unravel the enemy's messages.

The Navajo and other American Indians played a large role in such efforts. Military experts knew that their unwritten language was extremely challenging to decipher. In addition, it was only familiar to American Indians living throughout the Southwest. Navajo recruits created a dictionary of code words that translated to various military terms. About 400 Navajo code talkers acted as messengers in World War II. Their work was kept secret until the 1960s. They later became famous for their speed, accuracy, and dedication as they confused and frustrated the Japanese.

Just as important, the Navajo gained recognition for making a significant contribution to the U.S. war effort. For centuries American Indians had been denied the same opportunities as whites. Those living on reservations often struggled to receive a quality education and escape poverty and hardship. As the Navajo worked tirelessly to crack enemy codes, they therefore also waged another battle. They fought to prove that they were valuable citizens who deserved equality and respect.

CHAPTER FIVE
TRAGEDY
and Turning Points

The hatred and intolerance that shaped Nazi beliefs took on new and tragic dimensions in 1942. That year Hitler began ordering mass executions of Jewish prisoners in concentration camps, often using poisonous gas. Their genocide became known as the Holocaust. At first the world wasn't fully aware of what went on behind the camps' barbed-wire fences. Reports that trickled out were difficult to believe.

European Jews did not fit into Hitler's plans for an Aryan German empire. The Nazis devised a horrific solution to what they called the "Jewish question"—mass slaughter of Jewish prisoners. "We shall regain our health only by eliminating the Jews," Hitler noted in early 1942. Roughly 6 million Jews perished in Hitler's concentration camps.

Small numbers of Germans, ranging from Roman Catholic clergy to college students to Hitler's own officials, resisted. Some formed resistance groups or distributed anti-Nazi literature. Toward the end of World War II, a handful of German leaders secretly plotted to assassinate Hitler. After almost succeeding in 1944, many were discovered and executed.

The Germans forced the Jewish residents of Warsaw, Poland, into a small ghetto and by 1943 had killed them or sent them to camps.

But in countries controlled by Germany, fear frequently overwhelmed any potential resistance to the Nazis. Daring to speak out against Hitler's leadership involved great risks, as did helping people avoid or escape concentration camps. Opposing the Nazi government often led to imprisonment, persecution, or death.

While some Germans obeyed the Nazis out of fear, most others agreed with the party's ideas.

In other cases German citizens were swayed by propaganda. Nazi officials frequently blamed Jews for problems in Germany and the world. People used the arguments to justify carrying out Hitler's orders. A Nazi soldier wrote of his experiences to his wife. "I ... took part in the day before yesterday's huge mass killing [of Jews in Belorussia] ... When the first truckload [of victims] arrived, my hand was slightly trembling when shooting, but one gets used to this. When the tenth load arrived, I was already aiming more calmly and shot securely at the many women, children, and infants ... Let's get rid of this scum that tossed all of Europe into the war."

Up until spring 1942, the Axis powers had enjoyed little real resistance and a string of successes. The British suddenly took a more aggressive approach in May and launched an aerial assault on Germany. The Allies battled German general

U.S. bombers damaged the Japanese cruiser *Mikuma* during the Battle of Midway, and the ship sank.

Erwin Rommel in North Africa, fighting for control of the Middle East's oil. May also marked Japan's first defeat in World War II. The Japanese lost the Battle of the Coral Sea to U.S. troops.

Most experts consider the June 1942 Battle of Midway a huge turning point in the Pacific war. Midway Island is located roughly halfway between Asia and North America. Admiral Isoroku Yamamoto realized that Japan needed to push east to fend off future Allied assaults. Yamamoto planned to ambush U.S. forces at Midway.

Thanks to code breakers, Americans unscrambled Japanese radio messages outlining their intentions for Midway. The Allies were prepared for Yamamoto's advance on the island in early June. U.S. dive-bombers pushed the Japanese into retreat. After the Battle of Midway, Japan's reasons for fighting would be less about expansion and more about defense. Just as important, Midway marked a much-needed triumph for the Allied nations.

Yet World War II was far from over. Many of its most savage battles were still to come, including the Battle of Stalingrad. Historians consider it one of the bloodiest battles ever.

German soldiers in the Soviet Union were struggling to win control of eastern Europe. Soviet territories were vast and hard to conquer. Hitler's troops arrived in Stalingrad in summer 1942. If German soldiers failed to seize the city, they would soon be in the grip of a frigid Soviet winter while running low on food and other supplies. Consequently, German forces fought fiercely not only to help Hitler expand his empire. They also feared the pain of frostbite and starvation.

Stalin ordered the Soviets to stand their ground. If Soviet soldiers backed down in battle, they would be punished. They therefore proved ferocious defenders of Stalingrad, and vicious street fighting often erupted between the city's buildings. As

Stalingrad collapsed, Soviet troops forced residents to help defend their city. If anyone refused or fled, he or she could be executed on the spot.

Fighting finally ended in February 1943. By that point the Germans were out of supplies. Exhausted, hungry, and freezing, they at last surrendered.

The combined casualty count from the Battle of Stalingrad totaled nearly 2 million people. Yet the Germans had lost far more than soldiers. The Battle of Stalingrad represented a devastating humiliation from which they would never fully recover. Just as the Battle of Midway had been a turning point in the Pacific, so Stalingrad was a milestone on the European front. It was proof that Hitler could be overpowered. The Allied nations were no longer simply fighting to keep their enemies at bay. Moving forward, they would be fighting to liberate the world from Axis influence.

THE STEELY DICTATOR

Joseph Stalin was born Iosif Vissarionovich Dzhugashvili on December 18, 1879, in the village of Gori in southwestern Russia. Stalin studied to become a Russian Orthodox priest, but he became heavily involved in political groups that opposed the rule of Czar Nicholas II. He abandoned his religious studies in 1899 to plan labor strikes and other forms of resistance. Russian authorities banished him to Siberia in 1902. At about this time he began calling himself Stalin, which means "steel" in Russian. He eventually escaped exile and returned to Russia, where he worked to set the stage for the Russian Revolution.

Following the overthrow of Czar Nicholas II in 1917, Stalin gained increasing power under Communist leader Vladimir Lenin. He seized control of the Soviet Union when Lenin died in 1924. He rapidly banished or executed potential political rivals. The Soviet people learned to think twice before disobeying, threatening, or even questioning Stalin. His dictatorship was shaped by fear, violence, and famine.

After World War II, Stalin actively spread communism throughout much of eastern Europe. During the postwar years, relations with the United States were tense. Stalin died of a stroke in Moscow on March 5, 1953. Yet the effects of his ruthless leadership would live on in international affairs for decades to come.

CHAPTER SIX

CRUMBLING
Axis Influence

The course of World War II was changing by spring 1943. Combat operations in Europe, the Pacific, and beyond resulted in an increasing number of Allied victories. U.S. troops were still motivated by a desire to defend their country and defeat the Axis powers. Many Americans who entered military service were also young and deeply influenced by the patriotic energy that gripped the nation. Others enlisted to join family and friends who were already fighting in Europe and the Pacific.

The Allies forced the Axis powers to surrender in North Africa in May. From there, the Allies planned to invade Italy. It wasn't long before Benito Mussolini's troops scattered. The fascist dictator fell from power on July 25. The Italian people seemed relieved to be free of his rule.

> "I wanted to go to Europe with my brother ... [Training] was all marching, protocols, procedures, [and] policies ... It was tough: you're lost, you're away from home, and it's all new people, new procedures, [and a] new type of life."
>
> —Recollections of a female U.S. Air Force veteran

Patriotism motivated many young men and women to join the war effort.

Meanwhile, U.S. and British forces continued their intense air raids on Germany. The British Royal Air Force (RAF) struck the German city of Hamburg on July 28. The RAF dropped 2,326 tons (2,110 metric tons) of bombs in just 43 minutes. A combination of wind, low humidity, and warm summer temperatures set the stage for disaster, creating a firestorm that scorched Hamburg. As a Luftwaffe pilot later recalled, the blaze drained German morale. "A wave of terror radiated from the suffering city and spread throughout Germany," he wrote. "In every large town, people said: 'What happened to Hamburg yesterday can happen to us tomorrow' ... After Hamburg, in the wide circle of the political and military command could be heard the words: 'The war is lost.'"

Aerial bombing devastated Hamburg and other German cities.

Yet Hitler gave little indication that he agreed. Nor would he visit Hamburg to witness how the Allies had reduced it to rubble. But he was under attack from all sides. Italian officials formally surrendered to the Allies in September. Then in October they declared war on the Germans.

◀ Women Airforce Service Pilots (WASPs) flew supply planes for the U.S. Air Force, freeing men to fly combat missions.

For the rest of 1943, the remaining Axis nations would be forced to wage several defensive military campaigns. Through the winter the Soviets retook several key cities. And the Allies continued their efforts to weaken Japan's empire.

Just two years before, the Axis powers had cast a formidable shadow over much of the globe. Seemingly unstoppable, they had changed the

The Normandy invasion was the Allies' key to conquering Europe, giving them a place to land soldiers and supplies for the push east.

lives of conquered peoples throughout Africa, the Pacific, and Europe. But by summer 1944, the tables were turning. Now Japan and Germany struggled to maintain their grip on a fraction of the territories they had once occupied. The German fight for a more glorious empire and a better life appeared to have been in vain. With each Allied offensive, defeat became a stronger possibility.

Any hope of an Axis win was further weakened on June 6 when Allied forces launched an invasion code-named Operation Overlord. Better known as D-Day, it was a critical step in liberating western and central Europe from Axis influence. The plan was to secure the French coast first, attacking from the English Channel. Then the Allies could move inland to expel the Germans from central and western Europe. Allied commanders even developed fake plans to trick the Germans into expecting attacks at various locations. The true destination was 50 miles (80 kilometers) of fortified beachfront in Normandy, France.

D-Day was among the largest amphibious assaults in history. Five thousand Allied naval vessels landed in Normandy. The ships were supported from above by 13,000 warplanes. Roughly 160,000 Allied troops participated in D-Day.

Just before the assault, U.S. general and future president Dwight D. Eisenhower reminded the troops why they were fighting. "You will bring about the destruction of the German war machine, the elimination of Nazi tyranny over the oppressed peoples of Europe, and security ... in a free world ... Your enemy is well trained, well equipped, and battle-hardened ... [but] the tide has turned! The free men of the world are marching together to victory!" By July the Allies moved beyond Normandy and, in August, liberated France. At the same time, the Soviets fought to recapture eastern Europe.

Axis control crumbled throughout the European continent during the second half of 1944. Yet neither Germany nor Japan gave many signs of abandoning the war. Hitler still maintained power, and he clearly would not submit as readily as Mussolini had. In addition, fighting—even while at a disadvantage—seemed better to some Germans than submitting to the Allies. From World War I they remembered the hardship and shame that accompanied surrender. So both the will of their dictator and the bitterness of defeat spurred them on.

The Japanese made increasingly desperate attempts to beat back their enemies. Kamikaze pilots sacrificed their lives to dive-bomb Allied warships. In Japanese military culture, dying with courage was often considered better than living with the shame of defeat. Thousands of kamikazes took to the sky during World War II. Fearless and highly aggressive, they tended to be more destructive than traditional military pilots.

Young Japanese pilots gave their lives to try to salvage their country's war efforts.

Late October 1944 marked the first time kamikazes attacked Allied troops. During the Battle of Leyte Gulf, the Japanese attempted to fend off an invasion of the Philippines. Yet even the deadly efforts of kamikaze pilots could not defeat the Allies. After the battle ended on October 26, Japan's naval fleet was essentially in ruins. Without control of the Philippines, Japan was isolated from the rest of Southeast Asia. This severely limited the nation's access to essential supplies.

World War II was winding down. For some, the end would mean fallen empires. For others it would bring freedom—and new beginnings in a new world.

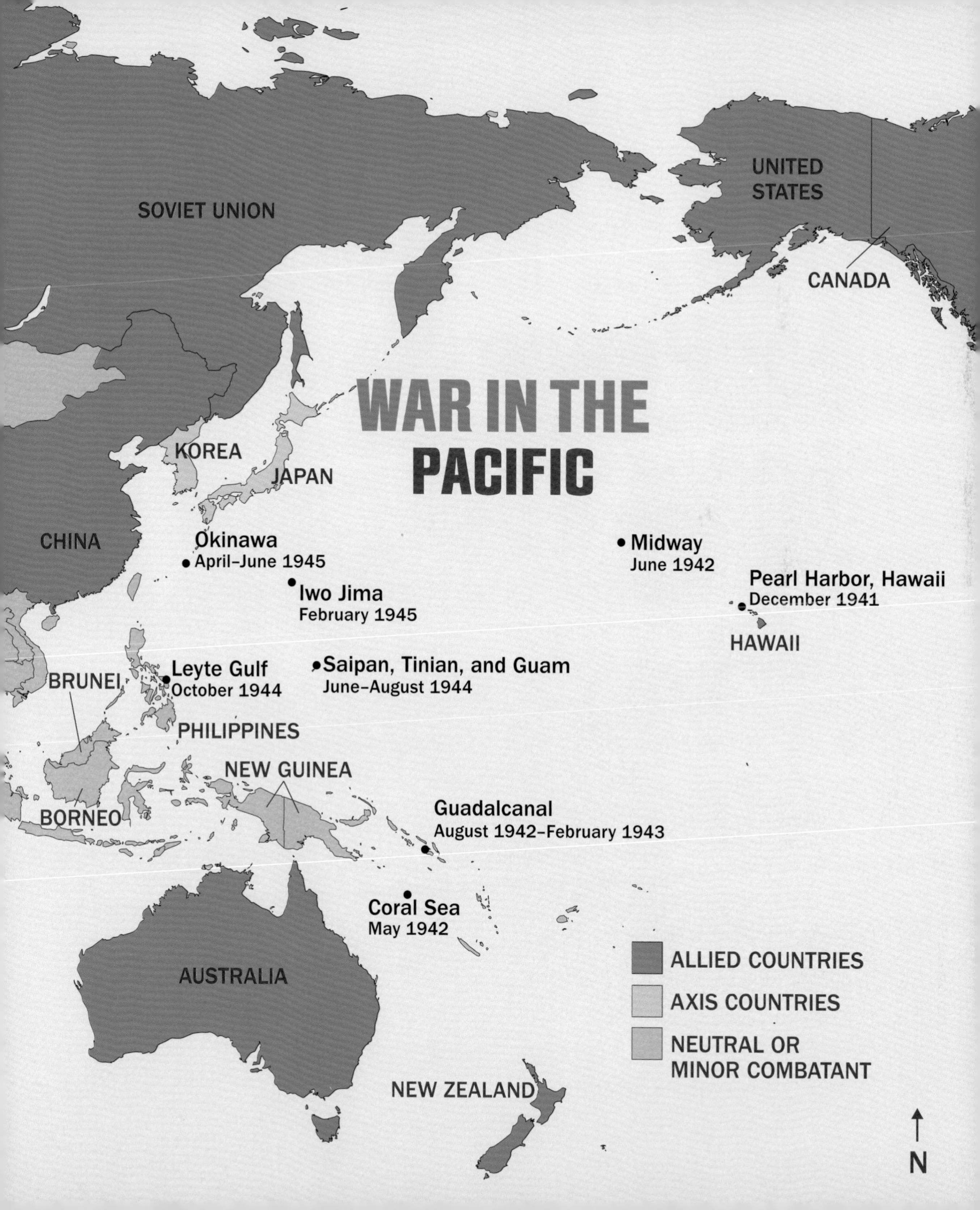

WAR IN THE PACIFIC

SOVIET UNION

UNITED STATES

CANADA

KOREA

JAPAN

CHINA

Okinawa
April–June 1945

Iwo Jima
February 1945

Midway
June 1942

Pearl Harbor, Hawaii
December 1941

HAWAII

Leyte Gulf
October 1944

Saipan, Tinian, and Guam
June–August 1944

BRUNEI

PHILIPPINES

NEW GUINEA

BORNEO

Guadalcanal
August 1942–February 1943

Coral Sea
May 1942

AUSTRALIA

NEW ZEALAND

ALLIED COUNTRIES

AXIS COUNTRIES

NEUTRAL OR
MINOR COMBATANT

N

CHAPTER SEVEN
PLANNING
For Peace

The outlook for the remaining Axis powers was grim in late 1944. Nevertheless, Hitler ordered a massive counteroffensive in Belgium, France, and Luxembourg in December. The Germans aimed to divide U.S. and British troops in northern France. If they succeeded they could then redirect their attention to the Soviets.

Known as the Battle of the Bulge, fighting temporarily created a bulge in the Allies' western line. There were at least 76,000 U.S. casualties, making it the bloodiest battle the United States fought in World War II. Despite the terrible loss of life, the Allies stopped the Germans and in January 1945 forced them out of Belgium, France, and Luxembourg. That same month the Soviets seized Warsaw, Poland. Meanwhile, the Allies progressed throughout the Pacific and pushed farther north in the Philippines.

Roosevelt, Churchill, and Stalin believed the end of the war was near. In early February they met in Yalta, a seaside city in the Crimea. During the Yalta Conference, the Allied leaders outlined their ideas for a postwar world. They also talked about creating a "general international organization to maintain peace and security."

A U.S. Army tank was ready to fire on the Germans at the Battle of the Bulge.

The "Big Three"—Churchill (from left), Roosevelt, and Stalin—met in Yalta to discuss ending the war.

The United Nations (UN) officially formed the following October.

They also discussed rebuilding Europe after the Nazis were defeated. The Allies strategized how to help liberated countries set up democratic governments. Germany would be split into various zones of occupation. France, the United States, the United Kingdom, and the Soviet Union would temporarily govern the areas. Finally, the Yalta Conference led to a promise of increased Soviet influence in both Asia and eastern Europe.

Japan and the Soviet Union had entered into a nonaggression pact in 1941. So the Soviets had stayed out of combat in the Pacific. Stalin was willing to begin battling the Japanese in exchange for a greater role in Southeast Asia. Roosevelt and Churchill agreed to Stalin's request. The leaders also decided the Soviets would exercise authority over eastern Europe. Stalin vowed in return to allow free elections in Poland and other nations liberated from Axis rule.

"We are told that the American soldier does not know what he is fighting for. Now, at least, he will know what he is fighting against."

—Eisenhower's remarks on touring a camp near Gotha, Germany

Following Yalta the Allies prepared to win what remained of the European front. They had captured or attacked the German cities of Dresden, Danzig, and Berlin by April. Hitler fled to an underground bunker, where he took his own life on April 30. Germany surrendered to Allied forces on May 7. The savage and historic conflict that had shaken Europe for more than five years was at last over.

As the Allies moved through Germany and its former territories, they encountered the Nazis' horrific concentration camps. Since the middle of the war, accounts of the mass killings that occurred there had become more widespread. Nevertheless, seeing the realities of genocide firsthand shocked even seasoned generals such as Dwight D. Eisenhower. The prisoners who had managed to survive the Nazis were freed, though their lives would never be the same.

If they were not murdered as soon as they arrived, prisoners of concentration camps faced forced labor, illness, and starvation.

Having achieved victory in Europe, the Allies concentrated on the Pacific. They inched closer to Japan. Yet the Japanese still controlled 1.8 million troops in their home islands. Even with Soviet support, the Allies perceived the potential for drawn-out fighting in the Pacific. This left the new U.S. president, Harry S. Truman, with a remarkably difficult decision. Truman had been sworn into office when Roosevelt died in April 1945.

In midsummer Truman met with Churchill and Stalin in Potsdam, Germany. During the gathering they continued the discussions that had taken place at Yalta. One result of the Potsdam Conference was a declaration warning Japan of "prompt and utter destruction." According to the Allies, the only way to avoid such a fate was unconditional surrender.

For the Japanese, this was unacceptable. By late July they were dealing with widespread hunger. With their naval fleet and air force in tatters, they also grasped the likelihood of an Allied invasion. But unconditional surrender represented more than the humiliation of defeat. Submitting without setting any terms would almost certainly leave Japan powerless in a postwar world. Further, the Allies had not indicated what "prompt and utter destruction" involved. On August 6, however, the words became far more than a vague threat when the United States dropped an atomic bomb over Hiroshima, Japan.

Scientists in the United States had started developing the deadly nuclear weapon in late 1941. Years later the war was still dragging on in the Pacific. Each side had already paid a heavy toll. To avoid a continued waste of time, money, and human life, fighting in Asia needed to end. Allied military experts debated the best way to invade Japan. They predicted that an amphibious invasion similar to D-Day would end in approximately 1 million casualties. To Truman the option did not necessarily seem preferable to a nuclear attack. Based on secret testing conducted in New Mexico, scientists knew atomic warfare would prove swift, powerful, and deadly.

The bomb's immediate effects included 70,000 dead men, women, and children. Another 130,000 victims would succumb to burns and illnesses related to radiation in the years ahead. Then, on August 9, the Allies launched a second nuclear attack. The atomic bomb that exploded over Nagasaki, Japan, initially killed 70,000 people. Within five years that number would double. By mid-August Japan was utterly devastated by nuclear warfare.

A day before the assault on Nagasaki, the Soviet Union had declared war on Japan. Eager to grab hold of new territories in Asia, Stalin dispatched troops to Manchuria. Knowing they were unable to do

battle on multiple fronts, the Japanese surrendered unconditionally on August 14. The Allies began occupying Japan's home islands by the end of the month.

Smoke from the atomic bomb rose 10,000 feet (3,000 meters) over Hiroshima, Japan.

Almost six years after World War II started, peace slowly settled across the Pacific and throughout Europe. The Allies achieved a clear victory, though at a high price in casualties. Allied nations had succeeded in halting Axis aggression on a global scale. They had either preserved or restored their freedoms and territories. The Allies also hoped they had set the stage for spreading democracy around the world.

In the short term, the Axis powers failed to achieve their goals. Dreams of German, Japanese, and Italian expansion were crushed. Hitler and Mussolini were dead. The Allies purposely destroyed factories and halted industrial growth in Germany and Japan. They reasoned that this would prevent Axis powers from producing weapons and other military supplies. Axis nations also lost any new territories they had acquired during World War II. The nations entered a period of financial hardship. Germany and Japan paid some reparations, but the Allies were careful to allow some economic recovery. Leaders, especially Truman, did not want to set up the postwar conditions that had followed World War I and had led to World War II.

The Allies annexed one-fourth of the land that had made up prewar Germany. What remained of the country was split into the zones of occupation discussed at the Yalta Conference. The Soviets also used the

Berlin was split between the Soviets, British, French, and Americans.

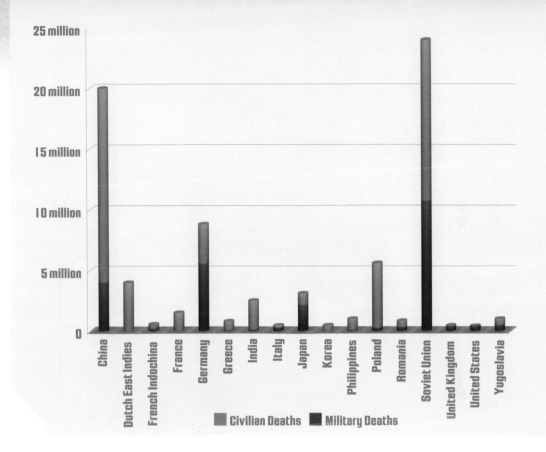

Civilian Deaths   Military Deaths

Yalta agreements to claim ownership of portions of Japan.

World War II left the Soviet Union a major world power. Stalin's influence was felt throughout much of eastern Europe. After the war he did not always honor his pledge to support free elections. For some central and eastern European countries, liberation from Germany simply meant occupation by the Soviets.

It took a long time for western Europe to recover from World War II. The British had fought to defend their freedom and prevent a full-blown German invasion. In that regard they succeeded. But the conflict had left the United Kingdom deeply in debt. And like so much of Europe, portions of the country had been completely leveled by bombs. The United States initiated the Marshall Plan, funneling nearly

$13 billion to western Europe to help the region rebuild.

The United States suffered less physical damage. Economically, increased wartime manufacturing had helped Americans recover from the Great Depression. Yet the end of World War II marked the start of new international concerns for the United States. From 1945 to 1991, Soviets and Americans engaged in the Cold War. The conflict featured no actual combat between the Soviets and the Americans. Yet it was a period of diplomatic and military tension between two world superpowers. The Cold War ended when the Soviet Union fell in 1991. Nations that had previously been controlled by a Communist Soviet government became independent republics.

World War II also reshaped social ideas and policies. The war prompted U.S. citizens to reconsider women's rights and racial equality. The fight to overcome discrimination would continue for years. But the war helped prove that gender and race do not determine intelligence, talent, or loyalty. It also prompted people across the globe to reflect on the horrors of the Holocaust and nuclear warfare. Today organizations such as the United Nations remain committed to promoting tolerance and peace.

The tragedies and terrors of World War II continue to shape international relations. Yet ideally they will also teach unforgettable lessons. By examining history and working together as a global community, people have the power to prevent World War III. Understanding why World War II was fought is an invaluable opportunity for future generations to avoid repeating the past.

◀ Sailors and soldiers celebrated their return home and soon created a postwar boom in the United States.

TIMELINE

September 1, 1939—Germany invades Poland, effectively triggering World War II

September 7, 1940—The Blitz begins in London

September 27, 1940—Germany, Italy, and Japan sign the Tripartite Pact

March 1941—Congress passes the Lend-Lease Act

June 1941—Germany invades the Soviet Union

December 7, 1941—The Japanese attack Pearl Harbor, compelling the United States to enter the war

1942—Mass killings of European Jews begin at Nazi concentration camps

June 1942—The Battle of Midway begins and marks a turning point of the war in the Pacific

February 1943—The German surrender at Stalingrad marks a turning point of the war in Europe

June 6, 1944—D-Day gets under way as the Allies launch a large-scale amphibious invasion of fortified beachfront in Normandy

October 26, 1944—The Battle of Leyte Gulf ends and results in the destruction of most of Japan's naval fleet

May 7, 1945—Germany surrenders to the Allies

August 6, 1945—The United States drops an atomic bomb on Hiroshima, Japan, and launches a similar attack on Nagasaki three days later

August 14, 1945—Japan unconditionally surrenders to the Allies, effectively ending World War II

GLOSSARY

annex—to claim authority over the land of another nation

casualties—people killed, wounded, or missing in a battle or in a war

communism—system in which goods and property are owned by the government and shared in common; communist rulers limit personal freedoms to achieve their goals

democracy—a government system run by officials elected by citizens

draft—a system that chooses people who are compelled by law to serve in the military

ethnic—relating to a group of people sharing the same national origins, language, or culture

fascist—a person who believes in a form of government that promotes extreme nationalism, repression, and anticommunism, and is ruled by a dictator

genocide—the organized killing of a large number of people

inflation—an economic state in which prices of goods and services continue to rise

nationalism—pride and love of one's native country, and a strong sense of being part of a particular national group

propaganda—information spread to try to influence the thinking of people; often not completely true or fair

radiation—powerful and often dangerous energy produced by nuclear reactions

reparations—payments made to make amends for wrongdoing

ADDITIONAL RESOURCES

Further Reading

Atkinson, Rick, and Kate Waters. *D-Day: The Invasion of Normandy, 1944.*
New York: Henry Holt and Company, 2014.

Peppas, Lynn. *Hiroshima and Nagasaki.*
St. Catharines, Ontario: Crabtree Publishing, 2013.

Rappaport, Doreen. *Beyond Courage: The Untold Story of Jewish Resistance during the Holocaust.* Somerville, Mass.: Candlewick Press, 2012.

Raum, Elizabeth. *A World War II Timeline.* Smithsonian.
North Mankato, Minn.: Capstone Press, 2014.

Internet Sites

Use FactHound to find Internet sites related to this book. All of the sites on FactHound have been researched by our staff.

Here's all you do:

Visit *www.facthound.com*

Type in this code: 9780756551711

CRITICAL THINKING USING THE COMMON CORE

Read a book or look online to learn more about World War I. Describe key battles and other important events in that conflict. Find a few examples of the military strategies and equipment that were used. Compare and contrast World War I with World War II. (Integration of Knowledge and Ideas)

Reread Ernie Pyle's memories of the Blitz on page 17 and the German pilot's description of the Hamburg firestorm on page 43. Are there any similarities between the two? What is unique about each account? (Craft and Structure)

Why might encountering Nazi concentration camps reshape the Allies' reasons for fighting World War II? (Key Ideas and Details)

SOURCE NOTES

Page 7, pull quote: Brian Murdoch. *Fighting Songs and Warring Words: Popular Lyrics of Two World Wars*. New York: Routledge, 1990, p. 121.

Page 12, line 8: "Ovation in London." *The Times* [London]. 1 Oct. 1938, p. 12.

Page 14, line 1: Robert Dallek. *Franklin D. Roosevelt and American Foreign Policy, 1932–1945*. New York: Oxford University Press, 1995, p. 250.

Page 14, col. 2, line 16: Winston Churchill. "Blood, Toil, Tears and Sweat, May 13, 1940." The Churchill Centre. 14 Jan. 2015. www.winstonchurchill.org/resources/speeches/1940-the-finest-hour/blood-toil-tears-and-sweat

Page 17, col. 2, line 2: David Nichols, ed. *Ernie's War: The Best of Ernie Pyle's War Dispatches*. New York: Random House, 1986, pp. 43–44.

Page 18, col. 2, line 9: Franklin D. Roosevelt. "154—Fireside Chat." The American Presidency Project. 14 Jan. 2015. http://www.presidency.ucsb.edu/ws/?pid=15917

Page 20, line 3: Franklin Delano Roosevelt. "The Great Arsenal of Democracy." American Rhetoric. 14 Jan. 2015. http://www.americanrhetoric.com/speeches/fdrarsenalofdemocracy.html

Page 22, line 20: Laurence Rees. *War of the Century: When Hitler Fought Stalin*. New York: New Press, 1999, p. 14.

Page 24, pull quote: "Oral History Interview with Roy L. McGhee." *Oral Histories*. The Harry S. Truman Library and Museum. 14 Jan. 2015. http://www.trumanlibrary.org/oralhist/mcgheer.htm

Page 30, pull quote: Lawson Fusao Inada, ed. *Only What We Could Carry: The Japanese American Internment Experience*. Berkeley, Calif.: Heyday Books, 2000, p. 72.

Page 34, col. 2, line 2: Norman M. Naimark. *Fires of Hatred: Ethnic Cleansing in Twentieth-Century Europe*. Cambridge, Mass.: Harvard University Press, 2001, p. 81.

Page 36, col. 2, line 7: Adam Jones. *Genocide: A Comprehensive Introduction*. 2nd ed. New York: Routledge, 2011, p. 239.

Page 40, pull quote: "World War II Women Veterans." Chandler Museum Public History Program. 14 Jan. 2015. http://www.cgc.maricopa.edu/Library/communityHistory/WW2%20Women%20Veterans/index-4.6.shtml.html

Page 43, line 13: Martin Bowman. *RAF Bomber Command: Reflections of War; Battleground Berlin: July 1943–1944*. Vol. 3. Barnsley, South Yorkshire, England: Pen & Sword Aviation, 2011, p. 21.

Page 45, line 14: Dwight D. Eisenhower. "Order of the Day." American Rhetoric. 14 Jan. 2015. http://www.americanrhetoric.com/speeches/dwighteisenhowerorderofdday.htm

Page 48, col. 2, line 15: "History of the United Nations: Dumbarton Oaks and Yalta." United Nations. 14 Jan. 2015. http://www.un.org/en/aboutun/history/dumbarton_yalta.shtml

Page 51, pull quote: Donald L. Miller. *The Story of World War II*. New York: Simon and Schuster, 2001, p. 521.

Page 52, line 19: "Potsdam Agreement: Protocol of the Proceedings, August 1, 1945." NATO. 14 Jan. 2015. http://www.nato.int/ebookshop/video/declassified/doc_files/Potsdam%20Agreement.pdf

SELECT BIBLIOGRAPHY

Bendersky, Joseph W. *A Concise History of Nazi Germany*. 4th ed. Lanham, Md.: Rowman & Littlefield Publishers, 2013.

Bowman, Martin. *RAF Bomber Command: Reflections of War; Battleground Berlin: July 1943–1944*. Vol. 3. Barnsley, South Yorkshire, England: Pen & Sword Aviation, 2011.

Dallek, Robert. *Franklin D. Roosevelt and American Foreign Policy, 1932–1945*. New York: Oxford University Press, 1995.

Inada, Lawson Fusao, ed. *Only What We Could Carry: The Japanese American Internment Experience*. Berkeley, Calif.: Heyday Books, 2000.

Jones, Adam. *Genocide: A Comprehensive Introduction*. 2nd ed. New York: Routledge, 2011.

Miller, Donald L. *The Story of World War II*. New York: Simon and Schuster, 2001.

Murdoch, Brian. *Fighting Songs and Warring Words: Popular Lyrics of Two World Wars*. New York: Routledge, 1990.

Naimark, Norman M. *Fires of Hatred: Ethnic Cleansing in Twentieth-Century Europe*. Cambridge, Mass.: Harvard University Press, 2001.

Nathanson, Stephen. *Terrorism and the Ethics of War*. Cambridge, England: Cambridge University Press, 2010.

Nichols, David, ed. *Ernie's War: The Best of Ernie Pyle's War Dispatches*. New York: Random House, 1986.

Paxton, John. *Leaders of Russia and the Soviet Union: From the Romanov Dynasty to Vladimir Putin*. New York: Fitzroy Dearborn, 2004.

Rees, Laurence. *War of the Century: When Hitler Fought Stalin*. New York: New Press, 1999.

Woodward, C. Vann. *The Battle for Leyte Gulf: The Incredible Story of World War II's Largest Naval Battle*. New York: Skyhorse Publishing, 2007.

INDEX

ABOUT THE AUTHOR

Katie Marsico is the author of nearly 200 books for children and young adults. Before becoming a writer, Marsico worked as a managing editor. She lives with her family in suburban Chicago.